BULLYING

Published in the United States in 1990 by
Gloucester Press, 387 Park Avenue South, New York, NY 10016

Printed in Belgium

Editor: Catherine Bradley
Design: Andy Wilkinson, Rob Hillier
Picture research: Cecilia Weston-Baker
Illustration: Ron Hayward Associates
Consultant: Pete Sanders

Pete Sanders is a head teacher of an elementary school and is working with groups of teachers on personal, social and health education. Angela Grunsell is an advisory teacher specializing in development education and resources for the primary school age range.

The photographs reproduced within this book have been posed by models or have all been obtained from photographic agencies.

Library of Congress Cataloging-in-Publication Data
Grunsell, Angela
  Bullying / Angela Grunsell
    p. cm. -- [Let's talk about]
  Summary: Discusses bullying, why it occurs and how it can
  be handled.
    ISBN 0-531-17213-9
    1. Bullying--Juvenile literature. [1.Bullying. 2. Bullies.]
  I. Title.
  BF637.B85G78 1990
  302.3'4--cc20
  89-28332   CIP   AC

"LET'S TALK ABOUT"

BULLYING

ANGELA GRUNSELL

Gloucester Press
London · New York · Toronto · Sydney

"Why should I talk about bullying?"

"When someone comes up to me and says for no reason 'I'm going to get you after school,' I start to panic. I think to myself: why are they getting at me? I'm terrified. I feel as small as a mouse and giants are onto me."

Have you ever felt like Kim who wrote this? Maybe you have threatened to get someone after school. It's hard to know what to do when you are teased, threatened or insulted. Are you brave enough to stop bullying other people?

Sadly, bullying doesn't only happen in the playground: it happens in families, at clubs and in the classroom. This book talks about what it is and why it happens. It may help you to think about ways of protecting yourself.

> Often children have useful ideas about how to change things and stop bullying.

"What is bullying?"

Bullying happens when you try to hurt someone else on purpose as a way of making yourself feel better. Bullies pick on people to try to prove how strong they are. Bullies come in all shapes and sizes: big and small, young and old. But all bullies get their way by making their victims feel at a disadvantage. Sometimes bullies pretend they didn't mean any harm: they may say "I was only teasing." But if you feel even slightly upset, then you have been bullied. Bullies set out to hurt people's feelings and sometimes their bodies and belongings. Bullies try to make you give them something you wouldn't choose to, or make you do things for them.

What do people get from bullying? They may take money for themselves. They may force their victims to steal or lie to get things for them. But most of all they gain a blown up sense of their power. They hope that no one will be able to put pressure on them and that they will look strong and tough.

Some children try to force others to do things that are dangerous.

ARE THERE WAYS YOU CAN STOP BULLYING?

Trying to understand your own feelings can help you to

judge when it is best to leave a situation

share what is happening with others

get on with others

see you don't have to be liked by everyone

look confident even when you are afraid

recognize how others are feeling

tell others how you feel without being afraid

stop going along with things you really don't want to do

judge when and how to stand up for yourself and others

"How do bullies get what they want?"

You already know that if someone tries to force you to do things you feel uncomfortable about, then you are being bullied. But how does bullying work? Bullies work on their victim's fear. They can do this in lots of ways. There are threats of violence when people say things like "I'll beat you up" or "My brother's a black belt and he'll get you." But there are lots of less obvious ways that people can make you afraid. They may say "We won't talk to you if you don't …" or "I won't be your friend."

We all need friendship and love, so it can be very scary when people say things like that to you, especially if you like them or want them as a friend. It's a cruel threat to use. If you have forced someone to do something, you can never be sure he or she is on your side. You can't trust someone who has bullied you to respect you as a person. If you really respect yourself and other people, you don't bully.

"How do bullies feel?"

You may be able to get your own way by bullying other people, but deep down you can't feel very happy if you think people fear you instead of liking you. Bullies try to put all the bad feelings they have about themselves onto other people. Many people who bully have been bullied themselves and believe they have to use force. Bullies can also be people who always get their own way. They may not know how to behave differently.

If everyone fears you, then you are the one who is missing out in many ways because no one will ever tell you what she or he really thinks.

It's not surprising that bullying is common. Just think of all the violence – both real and made up – that you see on television.

"Why do some children become bullies and others victims?"

We all work out ways of behaving and being ourselves by watching and copying other people. We also learn from the way in which we are treated. The way parents, teachers and older brothers and sisters treat you has a strong effect on you.

Some adults use fear and cruelty to make others do what they want. You may have been hit or made to feel bad by those around you. Adults do not always explain very well to children why their behavior is unacceptable or hurtful to other people. Some adults may have used you to do things for them, rather than helping you to learn to make decisions about your own life.

Children can learn things from adults which those adults did not intend. Some children become so frightened of other people's anger that they try to please everyone all the time. If you are always trying to please others instead of saying what you want you may be someone who can easily be bullied.

Small children like to dress up as mommy and daddy and act out stories they have picked up from people around them.

"I sometimes get bullied. Is there something wrong with me?"

Bullying often takes place when people get into groups or gangs. Sometimes boys or girls can be good friends when you're alone with them. But they can turn nasty and spiteful when they are in a group of other children. They seem to become completely different. You may wonder what you have done. You feel upset. You wonder what's wrong with you. But it may not be you.

There's nothing wrong with you when you get picked on in this way. Some groups will bother people for no good reason if it makes them feel better or stronger. To make you into an outsider they might say anything — you are too thin or too fat, too rich or too poor, too smart or too stupid. But the only real problem you have is the fact you are being bullied. You do not deserve this. It is never reasonable when this happens. There is nothing extraordinary about you. Everyone is different and that's what's so good.

When you feel upset by bullying, it
may not be a good idea to fight back.
Think if anyone can help you.

15

"What's wrong with groups of children?"

Perhaps you belong to a group of children? Being part of a group can feel great. You feel strong and good because you belong. You're the best … all of you.

There is another side to it. You want to prove you're really part of the group. You may not think carefully about what you do. You may get carried away by other people's excitement. You can feel stupid and ashamed afterwards if you've let yourself down and hurt somebody else. But you can influence other people in a group you are part of so that they don't do things you don't want to do.

> Groups can work together to get things done. Groups can share their happiness and strength to make life more enjoyable for everyone. They can include other people in what they do or help them.

17

"Why do some boys bully other boys?"

All boys are afraid of getting bullied by other boys. This is the most common form of bullying – at school, on the street and in clubs. Boys sometimes think that "real" men get what they want by using physical violence and that no one respects men who appear "soft." Some bosses bully their workers, some husbands bully their wives and children and some teachers are bullies too. The idea that boys and men should act brave like super heroes and not show their feelings has a harmful effect on all boys and men. Boys need to show their weaknesses as well as their strengths.

Some adults say things like "Boys don't cry." Of course boys need to cry sometimes. Realizing your real feelings and finding the courage to tell other people about them is helpful to everyone.

A girl bully can be just as threatening as a boy. Also, it can be less easy to convince adults and get them to take action about a girl bully, especially if you are a boy.

"Can girls be bullies?"

Bullies are more often boys than girls. Lots of boys and men bully women and girls. Men in groups sometimes bully women in public by embarrassing them with comments and crude remarks. This makes women self conscious. Some men call women stupid and try to make intelligent women look ridiculous. Of course this is upsetting. So it's not surprising that the same kind of behavior happens in some schools. Boys claim more space in the playground, make more noise and act all the time as if they are the only ones with a right to be considered. It's not fair.

But this does not mean that girls can't be bullies. Some girls do bully smaller boys and girls. They throw their weight around just like some boys do. But more often girls who bully do it in sneaky ways – by name calling or keeping someone out of their games. They may spread rumors about their victim or make hurtful, personal remarks.

21

"What about racist bullying?"

Racist bullying and name calling happens to many children in schools. Some black people in the United States are harassed on the street and in their homes. In some schools racial victimization goes on where Asian and Afro-Caribbean children get insulted and sometimes some European and Puerto Rican children also. It is just another example of children learning hurtful behavior from others. Some people just cannot respect the differences between themselves and others and don't want to recognize the similarities. They convince themselves they are better by putting you down.

If you are being bullied in this way at school, it is important to let your parents and your teacher know. Black people and white people at workplaces, in housing and in schools are working together to put a stop to racism and racial discrimination. Many schools are facing up to racism as a particular form of bullying and are prepared to confront it.

If you are having difficulty in getting help at school about racist bullying, you need to get someone outside school to help.

"What can we do about bullying in our school?"

In some schools bullying is a problem, in others it doesn't occur. It's all a question of how seriously the teachers, parents and children take the problem. Often children have some of the most useful ideas about what might change things because it is they who know what is going on and where and when bullying is taking place. When you start to work together to stop bullying things always begin to change.

That's why it's always important to let other people know if you are being bullied or if someone else is being bullied. Teachers and aides in your school cannot know that bullying is going on unless you tell them. You may feel scared by your parents' angry reaction when you tell them you are being bullied. You may also be worried by what will happen if they go to school and tell your teachers. However, if you tell, you are helping to stop someone from getting away with bullying and usually teachers are glad to be told.

Getting to know other people properly means being open about yourself. Children can learn a lot from each other.

If there is bullying going on in your class, perhaps you could get together with other friends and talk with the teacher about it. You may know that some of the children in your class, not you, are getting hurt. Sometimes bullying happens in the bathroom, at playtime or outside the school gates. Do the adults in your school know this?

Class discussions can bring everything into the open. If the teachers know that lots of children are feeling unhappy, they can work with you to have a class or school policy on bullying. Games and activities which allow people to get to know each other better and to listen to each other and work together can help. When everyone begins to express and share feelings about life at school, it gets easier to talk about what makes you feel uncomfortable. This can help children who bully to realize what they are doing to other people and make them less likely to keep doing it.

Bullying goes on in the adult world too. Some people's rights and safety – their jobs, their homes, their land – are not respected by more powerful groups, big companies or even governments. When people get together, first to talk and then to take action to resist unfair treatment, they can change things. There are lots of examples of groups of people working together to defend themselves. As individuals they would not have stood a chance.

In a place called Minamata Bay in Japan, the people of a small fishing village got together and stopped a large company from poisoning their water with mercury.

"Should I tell on bullies?"

Bullies rely on people being too frightened to tell on them. Protection rackets are so called because criminal gangs offer to protect a bar or restaurant from being smashed up. They charge a lot of money for this protection. People can be so frightened of what these criminals might do to them that they don't go to the police. Some people who should be giving care and protection to children in fact bully or abuse them.

Once you give into a bully, he or she will be back for more. Bullies will try to scare you into not telling anyone at all, but actually it is they who will feel ashamed if their secret gets out. Talking about bullying with someone you can trust is the best hope you've got of stopping it.

> Although adults can sometimes make things worse, there are people who will listen to you.

"What can I do?"

It is hard to know what to do if someone is threatening you or
constantly picking on you. But you know from reading this
book that giving in or trying to fight back are not the only
choices you've got. Being able to tell other people how you
are feeling, especially if you are upset or afraid, is an
important first step to making it less easy for bullies to get
what they want. Join together with friends to bring things
out in the open and get all forms of bullying treated seriously
by people strong enough to help you.

When you feel good about yourself, people realize they
cannot "get to you" easily. If you like yourself you won't
need to bully other people. You will know that you can
depend on yourself, but also that you can ask for help.

Sometimes you may have to choose carefully whom you
ask for help in dealing with a bully. In some situations you
might call in a social worker, the police or a community
organization. Sometimes the council or a trade union will
help and at other times organizations like local Human
Rights Committees, Unions and legal centers are the best
people to help you get your rights. When you are older you
may wish to join a pressure group and work with others for a
fairer world.

What the words mean?

bullying happens when someone hurts someone else on purpose.

discrimination occurs when people put certain people at a disadvantage.

feelings are part of you. Everyone feels happy, sad, angry, afraid, jealous, worried, calm, or confused at different times.

name calling is insulting another person by calling him/her something intended to be hurtful.

people's rights are what every human being needs to be able to live a full life. Enough food, a home, health care, education, love and consideration from others, work are some of them.

racism is the belief that certain groups in the world are superior to others.

victim is someone who is hurt or abused.

violence hurting other people or their property in a physical way.

Index

Photographic Credits:
Cover and pages 4, 7, 8, 10, 13, 15, 16, 19, 20, 23, 25 and 28: Marie-Helene Bradley; page 27: Eugene Smith / Magnum Photographers.

302.3
GRU

Grunsell, Angela

Bullying

$10.40

DATE			

© THE BAKER & TAYLOR CO.